Fundamental report
Mining Industry

Victoria Gold Corp.
CVE:VIT

E.E.J. Convens

Gaelic Victors

ISBN: 9781081147686

D/2019/14.286/3

Independently published

*Always do your own due dilligence before investing and
make sure your investment suits your investor profile.*

www.gaelicvictors.com

Table of contents

Disclaimer

Black Bull Assets and its staff do not give you professional, financial or investment advice. The content of these business presentations cannot be used to make investment decisions. Although every effort is made to ensure that the content is correct, we cannot guarantee the accuracy of the information or data displayed. Black Bull Assets and their staff are not responsible for your investment decisions. The information provided may not be relied upon when making specific transactions The content only reflects the personal opinions of our staff. When investing, you must understand the Inherent risks associated with stock trading and that you may lose your original investment partially or entirely. If you have doubts about an investment or a financial decision, you must seek expert independent advice.Permission is required if you wish to refer to data or information from this site. By viewing this site and videos, you agree to this disclaimer. Always do your own due dilligence.

Foreword

In times of geo-political and economic uncertainty, investors seek to protect their portfolios against financial events that may have a negative impact on their assets. The search for a safe haven invariably ends with precious metals. Gold and silver, for example, have always been real means of payment and will undoubtedly continue to be so in the future. As long as people have limitations in their search for precious metals on earth, gold and silver will always form a wealth protection for an investor's portfolio. Gold is the only natural means of payment with a lasting value. In the Roman Empire it was possible to buy 500 loaves of bread with 1 ounce of gold. Today you can still buy 500 loaves of bread with the same 1 ounce of gold, even though this is no longer common practice. In the Roman Empire it was also possible to buy a tailor-made gown for 1 ounce of gold, which still corresponds to the price of a tailor-made suit as we know it today. So, contrary to what many people assume, gold is not bought with the underlying idea of being able to take in a high profit, but as protection against inflation and an inevitable new (monetary) crisis.

Price fluctuations in gold are subject to the currency values that can change as a result of economic, ecological and geo-political events. It is therefore always the currencies that move in a volatile way against gold and not the other way around. So if you want to buy gold in order to make a certain profit, it is better to invest in the paper gold trade such as ETFs.

An investment in physical gold will protect your purchasing power while an investment in a gold mining company can be a great hedge for your portfolio. It is therefore physical gold and gold mining companies that should be a fixed value in an investor's portfolio.

The four fundamental pillars of a strong portfolio are:

1: physical gold
2: physical silver
3: gold and silver mining companies
4: value investments (dividend stocks and real estate)

As you can see, cash has no place in the above list. Before the 2008 crisis, cash had a certain value and a certain return could be achieved with a simple saving account. As a result of the intervention of the central banks, most saving accounts now provide virtually no interest or even a negative interest rate on savings. As a result, cash as an asset (added value) has become a liability (loss-making or a cost). Those who produce in the masses see the value of their product decline, and that is not different in the monetary system. Anyone who contributes massively to printing money dilutes the value of their currency. Also in the world of investors, this is not strange. A company that wants to raise extra money and issue new shares, dilutes the value of the existing shares, and therefore also the investment of the shareholders who already had these stocks in their portfolio.

However, the dilution of shares in companies is specific. In commodities, pharmaceutical and bio-technological industries it is often necessary to raise funds for the further operation of the company. These sectors are very investment -sensitive and still have a considerable risk, which is why banks are often reluctant to cover their investments by means of loans. For the investor in these sectors, this means that they are risky investments and that a higher return can be expected. However, things often go wrong and large losses are made. It is therefore important for you as an investor to spread the risk. This can be done in particular by diversifying your investments in different mining companies. This is of course subject to the required self-examination into the value of the company and into the capacities of the management.

No analyst can make guaranteed statements or predictions about the future of a company or about its price potential. There are too many indicators that are not specific to the company, but that can have a major impact on the functioning of the company. These includes natural disasters, political situations, economic crisis, financial crisis and trends. Even though these are not directly specific to the company, this does not mean that we cannot already take these factors into account in the company's analysis.

A mining company with a potential hedge against a inevitable new crisis is Victoria Gold Corp. With a history of ups and downs, this is a fascinating company that will be ready to cast its first gold in the very near future and can therefore be considered a gold mining company.

History

Since its foundation, Victoria Gold Corp. has come a long and arduous way. Weather influences and other delays have delayed the Dublin Gulch / Eagle gold project in the Yukon Mining district. It is roughly estimated that Victoria Gold has had a two-year assessment process, in addition to the fact that agreements had already been made with the First Nation of Nacho Nyak Dun. Subsequently, the licensing process for obtaining a Quartz mining licence was initiated.

During 2012 and 2013, the company was busy with both the financing of the project and the composition of a motivated team for its elaboration.

Victoria Gold Corp. had hoped to be able to start the construction of the mine after obtaining the quartz mining license (1). Initially, the company had planned to be able to produce after a construction period of 18 to 24 months (2).

Financing the project would be a daunting task. Victoria Gold sold their Relief Canyon project to Perishing Gold for 6 million US$. Shortly afterwards, the Cove project was also sold to Premier Gold mines for US$ 28 million. The Cove project had already progressed to such an extent that it was known that the project had an Inferred Resources of 355.253.44 tonnes at a 20 grams per tonne gold indication.

This accounted for 231,300 ounces of gold. By taking over the project, Victoria Gold's partner was also taken over by Premier Gold Mines. This partner - Newmont Mining - had a 51% interest in the Cove project since a positive Feasibility study based on at least 500,000 ounces of gold (3).

Silver was found

Exploration drillings from the drilling program at the nearby Rex-Peso site in 2011, which were announced in early 2012, showed that borehole 10 gave a result of 27.4 meters with a silver content of 382 grams per tonne from a depth of 102 meters.

Borehole 2 of the Peso vein showed 15.8 meters at an average of 82.8 grams of silver from 58 meters depth. The results also indicated other minerals such as antimony, zinc and lead.

The Dublin Gulch area is 646 km² and has 3408 claims (4).

Feasability Study

T he feasability study showed that it was possible to build an open pit mine with a low strip ratio of 1.45 to 1, which means that 1 tonne of usable ore can be extracted from a volume of 1.45 tonne of mined material.

Extraction of gold can be done by Heap-Leaching. This is a process that allows gold to be absorbed from the mined material through a series of chemical reactions.

Already in 2012 Victoria Gold could start building the open pit mine to be operational as a producer by the end of 2014. The Probable Reserves in the Eagle Gold deposit at that time were 91.6 million tonnes with a 0.78 grams of gold per tonne which accounted for 2.3 million ounces of gold. Due to high operating costs for running the mine, the company decided to do further exploration on Eagle Gold to increase inventory and to raise more capital to build the mine (5).

A new NI 43-101
Feasability Study

A Feasability Study of October 2016 indicated that the total deposit of the Eagle and Olive project together has 2.7 million ounces of Proven and Probable Reserves gold, from about 123 million tonnes of ore with a 0.67 gram gold content per tonne.

A new NI 43-101 study of the Eagle and Olive deposit from December 2018 gave an estimated resource of 208 million tonnes to an average of 0.66 grams of gold per tonne. The Measured and Indicated Resources, together with the earlier Proven and Probable Reserves, indicated a resource of 4.4 million ounces of gold.

The Inferred Resources were estimated at 0.4 million ounces of gold.

Metal value's

The following metal values are calculated at a gold price of 1398.0 US$ using an interim exchange rate on Tuesday 9 July 2019.

Proven and Probable Reserves:

123 million tonnes of ore with a 0.67 gram gold content per tonne has a metal value of 30.11 US$ per tonne. The total metal value is then 3,703,530,000 US$ or 3.70 Billion US$.

Measured and Indicated Resources:

85 million tonnes at an average of 0.66 grams of gold per tonne, is a metal value of 29.66 US$ per tonne. The total value of these resources is 2,521,100,000 US$ or 2.52 billion US$.

Measured and Indicated Resources are a fairly accurate approximation of what the resource is and after re-evaluation the metal value is 2,016,880,000 US$ or 2.01 billion US$.

Inferred Resources:

20 million tonnes with an average of 0.64 grams gold per ton-

ne is a metal value of 28.77 US$ per tonne. The total value of these Inferred Resources is then US$ 575,400,000.

As Referred Resources are a rough estimate, the metal value after re-evaluation is 201,390,000 US$ or 201.39 million US$.

The total metal value of of the resources is US$ 5,921,800,000 or US$ 5.92 Billion.

The management

For the management team of Victoria Gold Corp. It is not the first project they bring to live, altough it did not all went well as planned.

At the beginning of 2018, the management was overcome by the anger of a number of shareholders by issuing 250 million shares to finance the transition phase from developer to producer. This resulted in a dilution of almost 50% for the shareholders.

With some delay, Victoria Gold Corp. is on the eve of production and is expected to be able to cast the first golden doré somewhere around September 2019.

Financial parameters

Victoria Gold Corp. has not been able to make a profit during the period as an exploration company. This is normal as exploration companies can rely mainly on the trust (or goodwill) of investors. The sale of two other Victoria Gold projects has made it possible to further explore the Eagle Gold project and partly finance the transition into an open pit mine. Further financing was possible by issuing new shares. The Consolidated Financial Statements of 28 February 2019 and 2018 show a Quick Ratio of 1.49. This means that the value of the rapidly tradable funds is much higher than the value of the short-term debts.

The Current Ratio of 0.21 is very low and shows that the company can have problems making ends meet because it has little working capital. The net value of Victoria Gold is 291.577.479 Canadian dollars and the debt ratio is above 50%. The company is therefore vulnerable should direct problems arise.

The Return On Equity was negative in previous years but is now slightly positive. The ROE is currently at 0.04%. The fact that the company is on the eve of production means that we can put these figures into perspective. Victoria Gold expects to be able to cast the first gold at the end of September or at latest beginning of October. From then on, the company's results will take on other forms. The financial worries will decrease (apart from any unforeseen and unpredictable factors) with a positive effect on the ratios mentioned.

The lifetime of the open pit mine will be about 11 years with an annual production of 200,000 Oz. The All In Sustaining Cost is US$ 638 per Oz. Including Royalties, the All In Sustaining Cost is US$ 720 per Oz (6).

The total metal value of the raw materials is US$ 5,921,800,000. The total cost of mining 2,3 million Oz is US$ 1,656,000,000. Total profit margin of the mine will be somewhere around US$ 4,265,800,000.

In the run-up of the first 3 years production, the maximum price per share could rise to around US$ 5.17 (based on a gold price of US$ 1398.0 per Oz).

Currency conversion from US$ to Canadian dollar on 14 July 2019 gives a share value of 6.74 Canadian dollars. This represents a potential increase in value of almost 1700% (before tax).

Values and figures given are for information purposes only and do not constitute investment advice, please read the disclaimer on page 4 carefully.

Latest news

In June 2019 shareholder Osisko Gold Royalties sold its shares to Orion Co-VI, which owns 154.5 million ordinary shares. A fee of 0.46 Canadian dollars per share was paid, resulting in a premium of 15%.

Through this purchase, Orion has increased its stake in the company to 37%. The total number of shares owned by Orion is now 318.1 million.

On 9 July, Electrum Strategic Opportunities Fund L.P. decided to sell 70.4 million ordinary shares to Orion Co-VI for 32 million Canadian dollars. As a result of this sale, Electrum Strategic Opportunities Fund L.P. no longer holds any shares in Victoria Gold Corp. As a result, Orion Co-VI again has a larger share in the company with a total of 350.1 million shares.

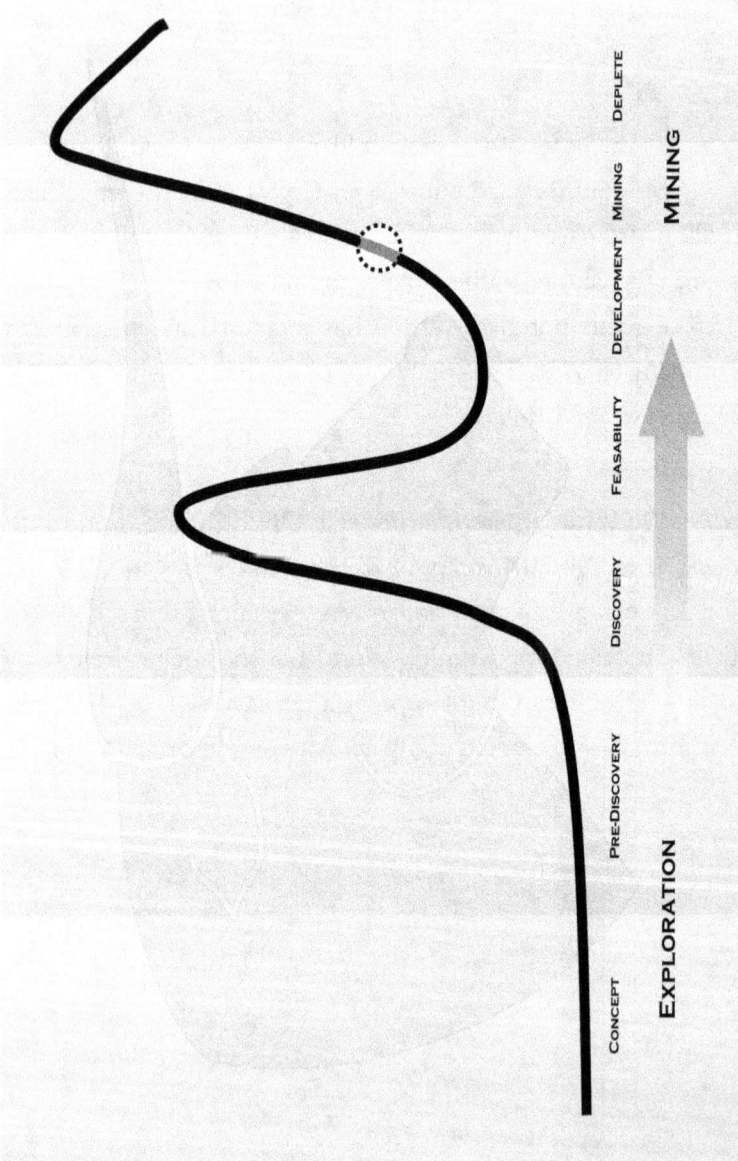

Sources

(1):   Northern Miner February 27, 2013 Volume 99 Number 3 Mar 4 - 10, 2013

(2):   Northern Miner September 24, 2012 Volume 98 Number 32 Sep 24 - 30, 2012

(3):   https://www.northernminer.com/news/victoria-sells-assets-to-focus-on-eagle/1001062404/

(4):   https://www.northernminer.com/news/victoria-hits-silver-near-its-yukon-gold-project/1000817869/

(5):   Northern Miner March 5, 2012 Volume 98 Number 3 Mar 5 - 11, 2012

(6):   https://www.vitgoldcorp.com/projects/development/eagle-gold-project/reports/

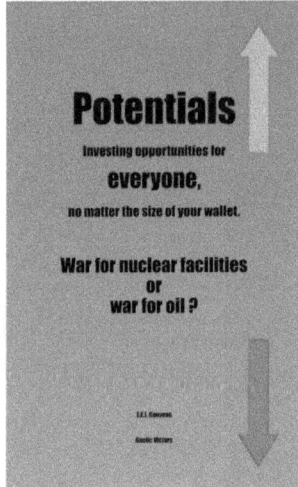

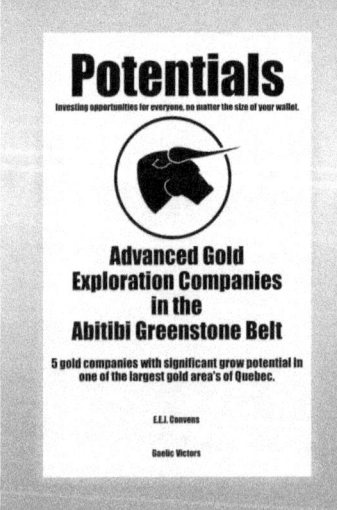

BLACKBULLASSETS.COM